Amazing Animals
Penguins

Please visit our web site at www.garethstevens.com
For a free catalog describing our list of high-quality books, call 1-800-542-2595 (USA) or 1-800-387-3178 (Canada).
Our fax: 1-877-542-2596

Library of Congress Cataloging-in-Publication Data

Arlington, Jane.
    Penguins / by Jane Arlington.—U.S. ed.
          p. cm.—(Amazing Animals)
      Originally published: Pleasantville, NY: Reader's Digest Young Familiies, c2007.
      Includes bibliographical references and index.
      ISBN-10: 0-8368-9101-5   ISBN-13: 978-0-8368-9101-0 (lib. bdg.)
      ISBN-10: 1-4339-2018-2   ISBN-13: 978-1-4339-2018-9 (soft cover)
      1. Penguins—Juvenile literature. I. Title.
    QL696.S473A75 2009
    598.47—dc22   2008013383

This edition first published in 2009 by
Gareth Stevens Publishing
A Weekly Reader® Company
1 Reader's Digest Road
Pleasantville, NY 10570-7000 USA

This edition copyright © 2009 by Gareth Stevens, Inc. Original edition copyright © 2006 by Reader's Digest Young Families,
Pleasantville, NY 10570

Gareth Stevens Executive Managing Editor: Lisa M. Herrington
Gareth Stevens Creative Director: Lisa Donovan
Gareth Stevens Art Director: Ken Crossland
Gareth Stevens Associate Editor: Amanda Hudson
Gareth Stevens Publisher: Keith Garton

Consultant: Robert E. Budliger (Retired), NY State Department of Environmental Conservation

Photo Credits
Front cover: Digital Vision. Title page: Corel Professional Photos. Contents: Dynamic Graphics. page 6: Digital Vision. page 8-9: Digital Vision. page 9 (lower right): Corel Professional Photos. page 10 and 11: Corel Professional Photos. page 12: Digital Vision. page 13: PhotoDisc. page 14-15: Corel Professional Photos. page 16 (upper left): Corel Professional Photos. page 16-17: Dynamic Graphics, Inc. page 18 (lower left): Corel Professional Photos. page 19-21: Dynamic Graphics, Inc. page 22-23: Digital Vision. page 24-25: PhotoDisc. page 26-27: Digital Vision. page 28 (lower left): Corel Professional Photos. page 28-29: Dynamic Graphics, Inc. page 30-31: Corel Professional Photos. page 32-33: Digital Vision. page 34 (upper left): Dynamic Graphics, Inc. page 34-35: Corel Professional Photos. page 35 (lower right): Digital Vision. page 36 and 37: Corel Professional Photos. page 38-39, 40: Digital Vision. page 40 (upper left): Dynamic Graphics, Inc. page 42-43: Corel Professional Photos. page 44-45: Graphics, Inc. page 46: Digital Vision. Back cover: Digital Vision.

Printed in the United States of America

3 4 5 6 7 8 9 13 12 11 10 09

Amazing Animals
Penguins

By Jane Arlington and Sharon Langdon

Gareth Stevens
Publishing
A WEEKLY READER COMPANY

Contents

Chapter 1
A Penguin Story

Freezing Facts

Antarctica is located at the South Pole. It is the coldest and windiest place on Earth! It is almost completely covered with thick ice. Hundreds of thousands of penguins live there.

It's the first day of winter on the continent of Antarctica. A group of emperor penguins huddles together for warmth. The penguins chatter and whistle. Soon the mother penguins will lay their eggs.

After a mother penguin lays her egg, the father penguin rolls it carefully with his beak from her feet to his own. Then he snuggles the egg under a special feathered flap to keep it safe and warm. He says good-bye to his mate. She sets off on a very long walk to the sea to find food.

The father penguin shuffles inside the **huddle**. He is careful not to let his egg roll off his feet. At last it is time for his egg to **hatch**!

Egg Shells

Penguin eggs can be white, tan, bluish, or greenish. The size varies according to the type of penguin. The eggs of emperor penguins are the size of grapefruits! It may take a **chick** up to three days to tap its way out of its egg.

When the mother penguin comes back with food, she calls out to her mate by singing a song. It is the song she sang to him the first time they met. When the father penguin sings back, she is able to find him and her chick in the crowd. Her little penguin peeks out from his special place on his father's feet.

The chick grows quickly. Soon he is too big to stay on his parents' feet. He joins a group of other chicks, snuggling with them to stay warm.

The little penguin's mother shows him how to clean his feathers. Penguin chicks are covered with a layer of soft feathers called **down**.

Feet First

After baby penguins hatch from their eggs, they stay in a special place on their father's feet called a "brood patch." It is cozy and warm under the feathers.

Birds That Don't Fly

Penguins are birds, but they cannot fly. They are too big and heavy, and their wings are too short for them to stay in the air.

After a few months, the little penguin and the rest of the penguin chicks have grown enough waterproof feathers to go into the water. They follow their parents on a long walk to the sea. There, they will learn to catch fish.

When they reach the water, the little penguin jumps in with his friends. At first, the penguin chicks are not good swimmers. They watch how the grown-ups use their webbed feet and stiff wings to push through the water. Soon the chicks dive through the water like their parents.

The penguins spend many weeks at the sea, eating. When the air turns colder, they know winter is coming. By now, the little penguin is no longer a baby. In a few years, he will become a father himself — and balance an egg of his own on his feet.

Wild Words

A **rookery** is the place where thousands of penguins gather to mate, lay their eggs, and raise their young.

Chapter 2
Comical and Amazing

Cooling Off

Penguins are **warm-blooded**. Their body temperature is almost the same as yours! When they feel too hot, penguins extend their wings. This allows the extra heat to escape from both sides of their wings.

A penguin's webbed feet help it steer in the water. Its sharp claws grip the icy ground.

Penguin Portrait

Different kinds of penguins live in different parts of the world, but they are all similar. They have black or dark blue backs and white undersides. Their short legs and webbed feet are set back so that the birds can stand straight up.

Penguins have other traits in common:

- The beak, or bill, is short and sharp—good for catching fish.

- The wings are short and the bones inside are flat to keep them from bending.

- The puffy chest contains strong muscles that provide power to the wings.

- The tail is used for balance on land and for steering in the water.

- A pocket inside the penguin's throat, called a **crop**, stores food.

- A flap of skin and feathers, called a brood patch, keeps the egg, and later the chick, warm.

Looking Good!

Like most birds, penguins clean their feathers. This is called **preening**. Preening is especially important for penguins after they have been in the water. Diving pushes the air out of their feathers and flattens them. Penguins need to fluff their feathers to help trap their body heat. As they preen, penguins rub oil onto their feathers with their beak to make them waterproof. The oil is made in a **gland** near the tail.

Feather Fluff

Penguins **molt**, or lose, their feathers once a year. It takes three weeks for new feathers to grow in. During this time, a penguin cannot go into the water, so it does not eat. A penguin uses up a lot of energy while molting. It often loses half its body weight.

Preening helps penguins keep their feathers windproof and waterproof.

Asleep on Their Feet

Some penguins sleep standing up. They may tuck their head under a wing. Penguins can also sleep in the water!

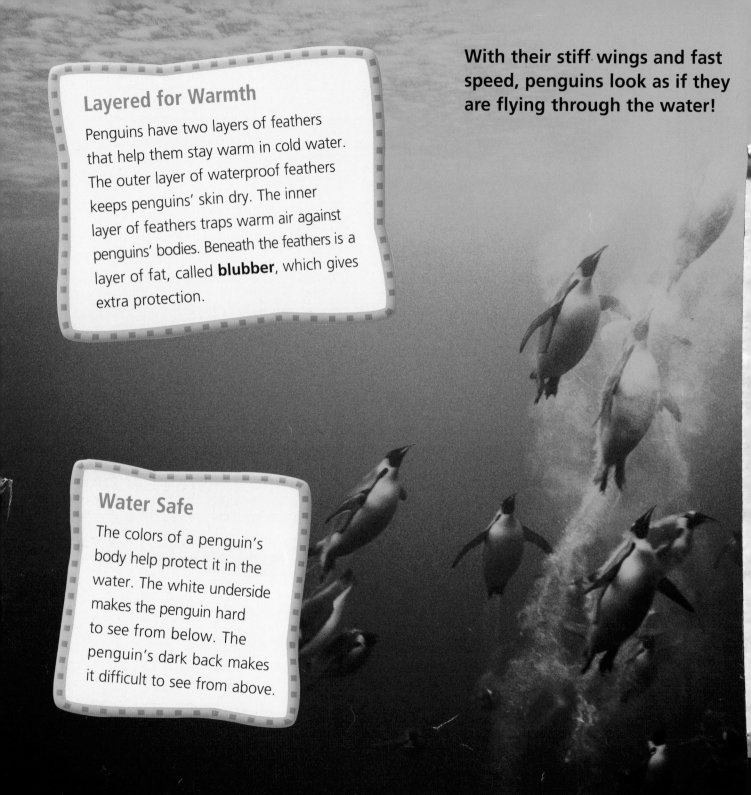

Layered for Warmth

Penguins have two layers of feathers that help them stay warm in cold water. The outer layer of waterproof feathers keeps penguins' skin dry. The inner layer of feathers traps warm air against penguins' bodies. Beneath the feathers is a layer of fat, called **blubber**, which gives extra protection.

Water Safe

The colors of a penguin's body help protect it in the water. The white underside makes the penguin hard to see from below. The penguin's dark back makes it difficult to see from above.

With their stiff wings and fast speed, penguins look as if they are flying through the water!

Birds That Swim

Penguins can't fly, but they are super swimmers. They are heavier than flying birds, which lets them dive below the ocean's surface. Penguins have a sleek shape that glides easily through the water. Their tail and webbed feet help them steer. Stiff wings act like paddles, pushing the penguins forward.

Penguins move faster in water than they do on land. Their average swimming speed is about 15 miles (24 kilometers) per hour — four times faster than a human swimmer!

Do Penguins Breathe Underwater?

Penguins can't breathe underwater. They must come to the surface to breathe air. Penguins swim for long distances by "**porpoising**." They leap above the water to breathe and then dive back in, as do dolphins and porpoises.

On the Move

Penguins spend most of their lives in the ocean. The rest of the time they are on land.

Since penguins don't fly, how do they get from the water onto land? Where the coastline is like a beach, penguins can walk onto land. But when the coast is rocky or high because of snow and ice, the penguins jump straight out of the water. They land flat on their feet, like cats. Adélie penguins can leap three times their height to get from the water onto land. That's like you jumping to the top of a swing set!

On snowy **terrain**, penguins "toboggan." They slide on their bellies, using their wings and feet to push themselves down hills and across the snow. On long journeys, penguins take turns being first. The leader flops onto its stomach and makes a track in the snow, which the others follow. This saves energy, because the other penguins don't need to create their own tracks.

Upstanding

Penguins are able to stand upright. Their legs are set far back on their bodies, unlike the legs of other birds.

Penguins often march in long lines like soldiers. They walk with their feet flat on the ground, swaying from side to side. It can look very funny!

Chapter 3
Group Living

Unique Voices

Different species of penguins find each other in huge groups by using different sorts of sounds. They include trumpeting, cooing, singing, and croaking. Parents and chicks also recognize each other by sight.

Huddling for Warmth

In the southern half of the world where penguins live, the seasons are the opposite of the northern hemisphere. For penguins in Antarctica, the harsh winter begins in May and ends around September. Summer begins in October or November and ends by March.

Living in large groups helps penguins keep warm. Emperor penguins form huddles during harsh winter weather. They take turns standing in the middle, where it is warmest, and on the outside where it is coldest. On extremely cold days, penguins huddle very close together. This reduces the amount of heat they lose by as much as 50 percent.

Wild Words

A **pride** is a large group of penguins.

Safety in Numbers

Living in a huge group increases a penguin's chances of survival against **predators**. One penguin does not pose a threat to an attacker, but thousands of penguins together are a strong show of force.

Leopard seals, fur seals, sea lions, sharks, and killer whales hunt penguins in the water. On land, penguins are hunted by foxes and snakes. One of the main threats to penguins is water pollution by humans.

Penguin eggs and babies are at risk of attacks from birds that swoop down from the air, such as **skuas**, sheathbills, and giant petrels. These birds usually attack chicks that have strayed from the group or that are weak or sick.

Beak Defense!

When penguins see a bird flying in to attack, they raise an alarm call to the colony. At once, thousands of beaks turn upward to the sky. Faced with this pointed defense, predators usually fly away.

Thousands of pairs of eyes are much better than one pair when it comes to spotting attackers.

Jumping In

When a group of penguins reaches the edge of the ice, they don't always rush into the water. Often, one brave bird jumps in first to make sure no predator is nearby. Then the rest of the penguins jump in, sometimes all at once!

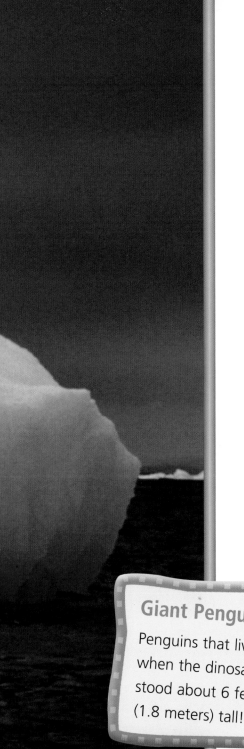

Sea Food

Penguins eat only when they are at sea. Penguins that live in zoos must be trained how to eat on land.

Penguins eat fish, crabs, shrimp, and squid. They also eat tiny shrimplike animals called **krill**. They have a big appetite. Swimming uses up a lot of energy. Adélie penguins eat an average of one shrimp every six seconds!

Penguins don't have teeth. They swallow their food whole. Their tongues are spiny and their jaws are strong. This enables them to hang onto slippery fish.

Unlike humans, penguins can drink salty seawater without becoming sick. Special glands at the tips of their beaks remove the salt. The salt flows down grooves to the end of the beaks and drips off.

Giant Penguins

Penguins that lived when the dinosaurs did stood about 6 feet (1.8 meters) tall!

Chapter 4
Parents and Chicks

Egg Sitter

Penguin dads, like this rockhopper father, keep their eggs safe and warm until the baby penguin is hatched.

Mother and father penguins share the responsibility of raising their little ones.

Going Home

Every year, penguins return to the place where they were born — to molt their feathers, mate, lay their eggs, and raise their young. Some penguins must travel long distances to their home. Scientists believe penguins use the position of the sun, stars, and familiar places along the way to find their home.

Usually, the males arrive first to stake out a nesting site. Most penguins build nests on the ground. They use pebbles, sticks, grass, and seaweed. Other penguins build nests underground. Emperor penguins do not make nests at all. The father penguin puts the egg on his feet and keeps it safe in a special place under his feathers called a brood patch.

One in a Million

A penguin finds its mate among the thousands of penguins in the rookery by listening for its mate's song. Every penguin has its own song, which its mate can recognize. When the pair meet, they face each other and weave their heads back and forth.

Penguin Chicks

After hatching from the eggs, penguin chicks stay on their parents' feet for warmth and safety. At about seven weeks old, most chicks are too big to stay with their parents. They join a nursery group of other chicks, called a **crèche**, where they huddle together for warmth. In some species, the crèche is guarded by adult penguins.

Young penguins depend on their parents for food — even after they have grown too big to stand on their parents' feet. They cannot enter the water until their fluffy down feathers are replaced by adult ones. Once the chick has fledged, or grown its adult feathers, it can go into the water to feed itself.

Feed Me!

A penguin chick's parents take turns going to the sea and bringing back food for their baby. The parent stores the food in its crop, a pocket inside the penguin's throat specially for this purpose. The parent **regurgitates** the food directly into the chick's mouth.

When young penguins
are too big to stay on their
parents' feet, they huddle
together in a small group.

Chapter 5
Penguins in the World

Wild and Crazy Feathers

Rockhopper penguins are named for the way they get around. They hop from rock to rock! They have a crest of feathers on the top of their heads with a plume of yellow ones. Rockhoppers live on the rocky islands of the sub-Antarctic and on warmer islands in the Indian and southern Atlantic Oceans.

Adélie penguins are named for Adélie Dumont d'Urville, the wife of the French explorer of Antarctica. They are the smallest of the penguins living in the Antarctic.

All Kinds of Penguins

There are 17 different kinds of penguins.

• Emperor penguins are the largest. They are 36 to 48 inches (91 to 123 centimeters) high, or about the size of a fourth grader! They live only in Antarctica.

• King penguins are the second largest and look a lot like emperor penguins. Kings have bright yellow feathers on their chest. They are about 37 inches (94 cm) high. King penguins live on the sub-Antarctic and Antarctic islands.

• Little Blues are the smallest penguins. They are only 10 to 12 inches (25 to 30 cm) high. Little Blues can be found only in Australia and New Zealand. Of all the penguins, they sing the most.

• Galápagos penguins live on the hot, tropical island of Galápagos, off the coast of Ecuador in South America. Galápagos penguins are about 21 inches (53 cm) high.

• Chinstrap penguins are named after the black line that runs under their chin. Chinstraps stand about 30 inches (76 cm) high. They live only in the Antarctic and have pink feet.

Where Penguins Live

All penguins live in the Southern Hemisphere, below Earth's **equator**. Many live where it is icy and freezing cold. Others live where the temperature is mild or even tropical.

Penguins are sea birds. They spend most of their life in the water, where they eat. Once a year, they return to the place on land (usually on an island) where they were born. There, they molt their feathers and raise their baby chicks.

Fast Facts About Emperor Penguins

Scientific name	*Aptenodytes forsteri*
Class	Aves
Order	Sphenisciformes
Weight	60 to 90 pounds (27 to 41 kg)
Height	3 to 4 feet (.9 to 1.2 m)
Eggs	1 each year
Lifespan	up to 20 years
Habitat	ocean, coastline of ice-covered Antarctica

Royal penguins have a crest of yellow feathers on their heads. Royals mate only on Macquarie Island, which is between Australia and Antarctica.

Glossary

blubber — a layer of fat under the skin of sea animals that keeps them warm

chick — a young penguin

crèche — a group of young penguins huddling together for protection and warmth

crop — a pocket inside a penguin's throat to store food

down — soft and fluffy feathers

equator — an imaginary line around Earth that is halfway between the North Pole and the South Pole

gland — a part of the body that makes chemicals an animal needs to live

hatch — to be born by breaking out of an egg

huddle — a very big group of penguins

krill — a tiny shrimplike animal living in the sea that penguins eat

molt — to shed old feathers and grow new ones

porpoise — to leap above the water and breathe in air before diving into the water again

predator — an animal that hunts and eats other animals

preen — to groom feathers or fur with a beak or tongue

regurgitate — to bring swallowed food back into the mouth

rookery — a place where thousands of penguins gather to mate, lay their eggs, and raise their young

skua — an Arctic bird that eats penguin eggs and chicks

terrain — ground or land

warm-blooded — having a body temperature that stays the same even when the outside temperature changes

Penguins: Show What You Know

How much have you learned about penguins? Grab a piece of paper and a pencil and write your answers down.

1. What is the name of the place on the feet where male penguins keep their babies?

2. How do penguins release body heat when they get too hot?

3. What is the layer of fat underneath a penguin's feathers called?

4. Why do penguins take turns being first in line when they "toboggan" on their stomachs?

5. What is another word for a very big group of penguins?

6. How many different kinds of penguins are there?

7. What is the name of the pocket where penguin parents store food for their chicks?

8. How are penguins able to find their mates in a huge crowd?

9. Where do Emperor penguins live?

10. Which type of penguin is the smallest?

1. A brood patch 2. They extend their wings. 3. Blubber 4. To save energy 5. A pride 6. 17 7. A crop 8. By listening for their song 9. Antarctica 10. Little Blues

For More Information

Books

The Galapagos Penguin. Endangered and Threatened Animals (series). O'Connell, Kim A. (Myreportlinks.com, 2005)

Penguins. True Books (series). Squire, Anne O. (Children's Press, 2007)

Web Sites

Penguins

http://www.seaworld.org/infobooks/Penguins/home.html

The SeaWorld Education Department offers this resource for students who want to know more about penguins and how penguins live.

The World of Penguins

http://www.pbs.org/wnet/nature/penguins/index.html

With video and background information from the popular PBS feature on penguins, you can find out more about penguins and see them in action.

Publisher's note to educators and parents: Our editors have carefully reviewed these Web sites to ensure that they are suitable for children. Many Web sites change frequently, however, and we cannot guarantee that a site's future contents will continue to meet our high standards of quality and educational value. Be advised that children should be closely supervised whenever they access the Internet.

Index